W9-BZP-570

Fire at the Triangle Factory

Fire at the Triangle Factory

by Holly Littlefield
illustrations by Mary O'Keefe Young

M Millbrook Press/Minneapolis

For John — H.L.

For my beautiful nieces, Pammy and Emily —M.O'K.Y.

Special thanks go to Vicki Revsbech
and Robin Brown—H.L.

Text copyright © 1996 by Carolrhoda Books, Inc.
Illustrations copyright © 1996 by Mary O'Keefe Young

All rights reserved. International copyright secured. No
part of this book may be reproduced, stored in a retrieval
system, or transmitted in any form or by any means—
electronic, mechanical, photocopying, recording, or
otherwise—without the prior written permission of
Lerner Publishing Group, except for the inclusion of brief
quotations in an acknowledged review.

This book is available in two editions:
Library binding by Millbrook Press,
    a division of Lerner Publishing Group
Soft cover by First Avenue Editions,
    an imprint of Lerner Publishing Group
241 First Avenue North
Minneapolis, MN 55401 U.S.A.

Website address: www.lernerbooks.com

Library of Congress Cataloging-in-Publication Data

Littlefield, Holly.
  Fire at the Triangle Factory / by Holly Littlefield ;
illustrations by Mary O'Keefe Young.
     p.   cm. — (Carolrhoda on my own books)
  Summary: Two fourteen-year-old girls, sewing machine
operators at the Triangle Shirtwaist Company, are caught
in the famous Triangle fire of 1911.
  ISBN-13: 978-0-87614-868-6 (lib. bdg. : alk. paper)
  ISBN-10: 0-87614-868-2 (lib. bdg. : alk. paper)
  ISBN-13: 978-0-87614-970-6 (pbk. : alk. paper)
  ISBN-10: 0-87614-970-0 (pbk. : alk. paper)
  1. Triangle Shirtwaist Company—Fire, 1911—Juvenile
fiction. [Triangle Shirtwaist Company—Fire, 1911—
Fiction. 2. Jews—Fiction. 3. Italian Americans—Fiction.
4. Friendship—Fiction.] I. Young, Mary O'Keefe, ill. II.
Title. III. Series: Carolrhoda on my own book.
PZ.L73587Fi 1996   95-31561
[E]—dc20

Manufactured in the United States of America
7 8 9 10 11 12 – JR – 10 09 08 07 06 05

Author's Note

In the early 1900s, New York City had more clothing factories than any other place in the world. The people employed in these factories worked long and hard—sometimes more than 10 hours a day, seven days a week—for very little money. Many of these workers were recent immigrants, and the only jobs they could find were in the factories. If they didn't work, their families would have no money to pay for food, clothes, or housing.

The conditions in the factories were unpleasant and often very dangerous. In those days, there were very few laws requiring safe working conditions. The factories were crowded and dirty, with poor lighting and little ventilation, and many of the buildings were firetraps. Often it seemed that factory owners cared more about making money than they did about the safety of their workers.

The Triangle Shirtwaist Company was located on the 8th, 9th, and 10th floors of the Asch Building on the corner of Washington Place and Greene Street in New York City. More than 600 people, mostly immigrant women and girls from Eastern Europe, Russia, and Italy, worked at the Triangle factory, making the fancy women's blouses called shirtwaists that were the popular fashion. The blouses were made from very thin cotton or linen fabric. This material was so delicate it would burn even more easily than paper. Despite this, the owners of the factory paid little attention to fire safety. Containers of sewing machine oil were kept near large bins of fabric scraps. Highly flammable patterns hung from wires on the ceiling, and workers nearby were allowed to smoke. No fire drills were ever conducted, and the one fire escape in the building was old, rickety, dangerously steep, and stopped two floors above the ground. But in spite of repeated complaints from the workers—who had even gone on strike to demand safer working conditions—the building was called fireproof, and it always passed its safety inspections.

On Saturday, March 25, 1911, a fire started on the eighth floor, in the Triangle factory. This is the story of two young girls caught in that fire. Although the characters are fictional, the events that take place are based on the actual accounts of those who survived the fire.

March 25, 1911

Minnie Levine ran down the steps
of her building to the street.
Spring would come soon
to New York City.
But it was still cold outside.
Minnie was early today.
The sun had not come up yet.
She rubbed her hands together.
She walked as fast as she could
to keep warm.

The street was almost empty.
All the shops Minnie passed
were closed.
It was Saturday, the Jewish Sabbath.

In Minnie's neighborhood,
people were supposed to rest.
But most of the factories
didn't close on Saturdays.
Minnie worked at the
Triangle Shirtwaist Company.
She made fancy blouses
called shirtwaists.

Minnie had started at the factory
when she was 10.
Her job then was to cut loose threads
off the finished blouses.
Children that young were not
supposed to work in factories.
When an inspector came, Minnie
would hide in a big bin of cloth.
So would the other girls her age.
Minnie and her best friend, Tessa,
would hide together in one bin.
They knew they would lose their jobs
if the inspector found them.
Now Minnie was 14.
She didn't have to hide anymore.
She had a more important job, too.
Both Minnie and Tessa
were sewing machine operators.

They had to be at work by 7:15.
Sometimes the day didn't end
until after 5:00, 10 hours later.
The Triangle factory was at
the corner of Washington Place
and Greene Street.

It was a very long walk.

But Minnie liked it.

It gave her a chance to talk to Tessa.

Minnie's papa would be angry

if he knew Tessa was her friend.

Papa grew up in Poland.

A Jewish girl could never be friends

with a Catholic girl there.

Papa didn't understand that

in America things were different.

Minnie turned the corner
of Tessa's street.
In Tessa's Italian neighborhood,
the holy day was Sunday.
Here the shops were open.
The streets were busy with people
getting ready for work.

Tessa was waiting
in front of her building.
She smiled when she saw Minnie.
"I was afraid you wouldn't come
this morning," Tessa said.
"It's so cold.
I thought you might take the trolley."
"No," Minnie said.
"I wanted to walk with you."

At the factory, the girls rode
the elevator to the ninth floor.
They put their wraps away.
Then they went out to the workroom.
At 7:30, the power was turned on.
The sewing machines
began to whir and hum.
It sounded like the inside
of a giant beehive.
It was so loud that Minnie and Tessa
had to shout to hear each other.

But this didn't matter
because talking wasn't allowed.
The big room was filled
with rows of tables.
Each table had a long line
of sewing machines on it.
The girls and women who
ran the machines sat side by side.
The room was so crowded that
sometimes the workers'
shoulders would touch.

The floor was covered with pieces of
cloth and shirtwaist patterns.
Finished work hung from the ceiling.
Sewing machine oil was everywhere.
Everyone knew that a fire
could easily start.
There had already been two small
fires since Minnie had worked there.
Some of the workers had said
they wouldn't work unless
the problems were fixed.
The bosses promised to make
the factory safer.
But they didn't keep their promises.

Minnie had to work very carefully.
If she didn't, she could catch
her finger under the needle
of her sewing machine.
Or she might tear the thin
cotton cloth she was working on.
She earned only six dollars a week.
But if she hurt any of the cloth
or broke her needle,
she would have to pay for it.

Minnie's family needed
every penny she made.
They had to pay rent and buy food.
Minnie wished she could
go to school like her brothers.
But there wasn't enough
money for that.
Minnie's father had a job
loading ships.
Her mother made some money
sewing at home.
But even with the money Minnie
made, the family was very poor.

It was almost 5:00.
The sewing machines
had been turned off.
The workers were getting ready
to go home.
Suddenly, Minnie heard
glass breaking.
"Fire!" someone yelled.

Minnie looked up
and almost screamed.
She saw flames in the windows.
The fire was moving quickly.
It was burning through
the piles of cloth that filled the room.
This fire seemed much bigger than
the others Minnie had seen.

The room was filling with smoke.
People tried to run from the fire.
But the rows between the sewing
machines were narrow and crowded.
It was hard to get through.
Some of the women tried to jump
across the tops of the tables.
But they tripped over the
sewing machines and cloth.
People were pushing and screaming.
Minnie looked at Tessa.
Tessa was so frightened,
she couldn't move.
Minnie grabbed her friend's hand.
"This way!" she yelled.
Minnie dropped to her
hands and knees and began
to crawl under the tables.

Tessa followed her.

It was hard to squeeze through
the chairs and table legs.

But they finally reached the edge
of the big room.

"Come on!" Minnie yelled.

She pointed toward the elevators.

There were dozens of women
in front of the elevators.
When the doors opened, almost
everyone tried to get on.
The elevators were only meant
to carry about 10 people at a time.
Minnie and Tessa watched
as more than 30 women
shoved their way into
one elevator.
Some people were so scared
they stepped on other people
to get to safety.
"Let's try the stairs instead,"
Minnie said.

Minnie's eyes and throat
were stinging from the smoke.
She could barely see.
Suddenly, Minnie felt something
burning against her legs.
She looked down and cried out.
Her dress was on fire!
Minnie spun around, slapping at
the flames with her hands.
Tessa screamed for help.
But no one could hear her
above the noise of the fire.
She had to save Minnie!
Then Tessa saw a bucket of water
hanging from the wall.
She grabbed it and threw
the water at Minnie.
The fire went out.

"Are you all right?" Tessa cried.

Minnie's face was covered
with tears.

But she nodded.

"Come on, then!" Tessa yelled.

"We have to get out of here!"

There was a crowd of people
in front of the stairway door.
"It's locked!" one woman cried.
She beat her fists against the door.
"They've locked us in."
Minnie remembered that the foreman
always locked that door
near the end of the day.
The bosses wanted to be sure
that no one tried to leave early
or steal anything.
Now that locked door was keeping
the workers from escaping the fire.

The smoke was getting thicker.

People were coughing.

They couldn't breathe.

Some of them ran to the windows
and broke the glass.

They tried to escape from the fire
by jumping out.

But they were nine floors up.

Minnie knew no one could
survive that fall.

"We have to try the other stairway!"
Tessa yelled.

They crawled through the smoke
to the other stairway.
The door was open.
The girls ran down the stairs.
Suddenly, fire filled the stairway
in front of them.
"Go back up, Tessa," Minnie yelled.
"Go to the roof!"
They turned and ran as fast as they
could back up the stairs.
The stairway was as hot as an oven.
The girls gasped for air
as they climbed.
Tessa tripped and fell.
But Minnie grabbed her hand
and helped her up the last few steps.
They finally burst through the door
onto the roof.

Minnie and Tessa gulped in
deep breaths of fresh air.
"Over here, girls," someone called.
Some other workers had also run
to the roof.
They were standing at the
edge of the building.

Next door was a university.
Some students lowered ladders
from their building to the roof
of the burning building.
"Hurry!" the students called.
"Climb up here.
Then you'll be safe."
Minnie was afraid.
But she knew they would have
to climb that ladder
to get away from the fire.

The students held the ladder steady.
One by one, the people on the roof
crossed over.
Minnie's hands shook as she
climbed the ladder.
"Don't look down,"
one of the students said.
Minnie closed her eyes tightly.
She was too afraid to look down.
Minnie carefully clutched each rung.
Finally, she felt hands
around her waist.

She opened her eyes as one of the
students lifted her off the ladder.
Tessa came after her.
Then Minnie and Tessa followed
the students through the building
and out to the street.

There were people everywhere.
Policemen tried to hold back the
people who had come to see the fire.
Hoses and ladders filled the street.
Many people had been hurt
by the fire.
Most of the girls who had jumped
from the windows had been killed
by the fall.
Suddenly, Tessa stumbled
and grabbed Minnie's arm.
"What's wrong, Tessa?"
asked Minnie.
"I hurt my ankle in the stairway,"
Tessa said.

There were tears in her eyes.

"I hardly noticed it then.

But now I don't think I can walk

much farther.

How will I get home?"

Minnie sat down next to her friend.

"Don't worry, Tessa," Minnie said.

"I'll get you home."

Minnie was worried, though.

She knew she couldn't carry Tessa

all the way home.

Just then, Minnie heard a voice
call her name.
She looked up.
It was her papa.
He picked Minnie up and held her close.
She hugged him and cried.
It felt good to be safe in his arms.
"Oh, Papa, I was so scared," she said.
He pushed her hair back from her face.
"There, Minnie.
It's all right now," he said.
"I came as fast as I could.
I was so worried about you.
Let's go home."

"Papa," Minnie said.

"I can't leave my friend Tessa here.

She can't walk.

I said I would help her get home
to Mulberry Street."

Minnie looked up at her father.

She knew he would be angry.

He had told her over and over not

to go to the Italian neighborhoods.

He had told her not to speak to

any Catholics at work.

Her father frowned.

"Minnie," he said.

"I'm sure some of her own people

can help this girl."

"No, Papa," Minnie said.

"Tessa is my friend.

She saved my life.

My dress caught on fire

and she put it out.

Please, Papa.

She needs our help."

"This Italian girl saved you
from the fire?" he asked.

"Yes, Papa," Minnie said.

Minnie's father said nothing.
He just looked long and hard
at Tessa.

Tessa looked up at him and smiled.
Then she held out her hand.

"I'm pleased to meet you, Sir,"
she said shyly.

"My name is Tessa Monnetti."
Minnie saw the frown on her
father's face slowly disappear.
He reached out and took
Tessa's hand.

"I thank you, Miss Monnetti,
for saving my Minnie," he said.
"Let me help you home."
"I don't want to be any trouble,"
Tessa said.
"It is no trouble at all," he answered.
"I am always glad to help a friend."

He leaned over and carefully
picked up Tessa.
Then they began to walk
toward home.

Afterword

In less than half an hour, 146 of the workers at the Triangle Shirtwaist Company—some as young as 14 years old—were dead. Most were killed by fire and smoke. More than 40 people jumped from the eighth and ninth floors of the factory. They fell to their deaths, crushed on the sidewalk below.

Afterward, people were angry that a fire like this could have happened. Why weren't there more fire escapes? Why were the doors locked? How come so many had to die? In the trial that followed, the factory owners were found innocent of any wrongdoing. The Triangle factory had met all the safety conditions required by law.

It became clear to many people that the laws needed to be changed. Now factories must have fire alarms, multiple exits, fire escapes, and sprinklers that automatically shower water on a fire. They are also required to conduct fire drills so that workers will know how to escape if a fire breaks out. It might not be possible to prevent factory fires completely, but perhaps because of the fire at the Triangle factory, never again will so many people have to die in one.